LIFE
Lessons
WITH MAX LUCADO

BOOKS OF 1 & 2 THESSALONIANS

TRANSCENDENT LIVING IN A TRANSIENT WORLD

MAX LUCADO

Prepared by

THE LIVINGSTONE CORPORATION

Published by
THOMAS NELSON™
Since 1798
www.thomasnelson.com

Life Lessons with Max Lucado—Books of 1 & 2 Thessalonians

Copyright © by Thomas Nelson, 2007

Published in Nashville, Tennessee. Thomas Nelson is a trademark of Thomas Nelson, Inc.

Thomas Nelson, Inc. titles may be purchased in bulk for educational, business, fundraising, or sales promotional use. For information, please email SpecialMarkets@ThomasNelson.com.

Scripture passages taken from:
Contemporary English Version (CEV). Copyright © 1995, American Bible Society.
The Holy Bible, New Century Version (NCV). Copyright ©1987, 1988, 1991 by Word Publishing. All rights reserved.
The HOLY BIBLE, NEW INTERNATIONAL VERSION® (NIV). Copyright © 1973, 1978, 1984 by International Bible Society. Used by permission of Zondervan Publishing House. All rights reserved. The "NIV" and "New International Version" trademarks are registered in the United States Patent and Trademark Office by International Bible Society. Use of either trademark requires the permission of International Bible Society.
The Holy Bible, New King James Version (NKJV). Copyright © 1979, 1980, 1982 by Thomas Nelson. All rights reserved.
The *Holy Bible,* New Living Translation (NLT). Copyright © 1996, 2004. Used by permission of Tyndale House Publishers, Inc., Wheaton, Illinois 60189. All rights reserved.
The Jerusalem Bible (TJB) Copyright © 1968 by Darton, Longman, & Todd, Ltd.,Doubleday & Co, Inc.
Verses marked TLB are taken from *The Living Bible* copyright © 1971. Used by permission of Tyndale House Publishers, Inc., Wheaton, Illinois 60189. All rights reserved.
THE MESSAGE (MSG). Copyright © 1993, 1994, 1995, 1996, 2000, 2001, 2002. Used by permission of NavPress Publishing Group.
The *Today's English Version* Bible (TEV). Copyright © 1976, 1992, American Bible Society. Used by permission. All rights reserved.

Material for the "Inspiration" sections taken from the following books:
America Looks Up. Copyright © 2001 by Max Lucado. W Publishing Group, a Division of Thomas Nelson, Inc., Nashville, Tennessee
And the Angels Were Silent.. Copyright © 2004 by Max Lucado. W Publishing Group, a Division of Thomas Nelson, Inc., Nashville, Tennessee.
Come Thirsty. Copyright © 2004 by Max Lucado. W Publishing Group, a Division of Thomas Nelson, Inc., Nashville, Tennessee.
Cure for the Common Life. Copyright © 2005 by Max Lucado. W Publishing Group, a Division of Thomas Nelson, Inc., Nashville, Tennessee.
A Gentle Thunder. Copyright © 1995 by Max Lucado. W Publishing Group, a Division of Thomas Nelson, Inc., Nashville, Tennessee.
The Great House of God. Copyright © 1997 by Max Lucado. W Publishing Group, a Division of Thomas Nelson, Inc., Nashville, Tennessee.
It's Not About Me. Copyright © 2004 by Max Lucado. Integrity Publishers, Brentwood, Tennessee.
Just Like Jesus. Copyright © 1998 by Max Lucado. W Publishing Group, a Division of Thomas Nelson, Inc., Nashville, Tennessee.
On the Anvil. Copyright © 1985 by Max Lucado. Tyndale House Publishers, Inc., Wheaton, Illinois.
When Christ Comes. Copyright © 1999 by Max Lucado. W Publishing Group, a Division of Thomas Nelson, Inc., Nashville, Tennessee.
When God Whispers Your Name. Copyright © 1994, 1999 by Max Lucado. W Publishing Group, a Division of Thomas Nelson, Inc., Nashville, Tennessee.

Produced with the assistance of the Livingstone Corporation. Project staff include Jake Barton, Joel Bartlett, Andy Culbertson, Will Reaves, Mary Horner Collins, and Rachel Hawkins
Editor: Len Woods
Cover Art and Interior Design by Kirk Luttrell of the Livingstone Corporation
Interior Composition by Rachel Hawkins of the Livingstone Corporation

ISBN-10: 1-4185-0974-4
ISBN-13: 978-1-4185-0974-3

Printed in the United States of America.
07 08 RRD 9 8 7 6 5 4 3 2 1

LIFE *Lessons*

WITH MAX LUCADO

CONTENTS

HOW TO STUDY THE BIBLE

This is a peculiar book you are holding. Words crafted in another language. Deeds done in a distant era. Events recorded in a far-off land. Counsel offered to a foreign people. This is a peculiar book.

It's surprising that anyone reads it. It's too old. Some of its writings date back five thousand years. It's too bizarre. The book speaks of incredible floods, fires, earthquakes, and people with supernatural abilities. It's too radical. The Bible calls for undying devotion to a carpenter who called himself God's Son.

Logic says this book shouldn't survive. Too old, too bizarre, too radical.

The Bible has been banned, burned, scoffed, and ridiculed. Scholars have mocked it as foolish. Kings have branded it as illegal. A thousand times over, the grave has been dug and the dirge has begun, but somehow the Bible never stays in the grave. Not only has it survived; it has thrived. It is the single most popular book in all of history. It has been the best-selling book in the world for years!

There is no way on earth to explain it. Which perhaps is the only explanation. The answer? The Bible's durability is not found on earth; it is found in heaven. For the millions who have tested its claims and claimed its promises, there is but one answer: the Bible is God's book and God's voice.

As you read it, you would be wise to give some thought to two questions. What is the purpose of the Bible? and How do I study the Bible? Time spent reflecting on these two issues will greatly enhance your Bible study.

What is the purpose of the Bible?

Let the Bible itself answer that question.

Since you were a child you have known the Holy Scriptures which are able to make you wise. And that wisdom leads to salvation through faith in Christ Jesus. (2 Tim. 3:15 NCV)

The purpose of the Bible? Salvation. God's highest passion is to get his children home. His book, the Bible, describes his plan of salvation. The purpose of the Bible is to proclaim God's plan and passion to save his children.

That is the reason this book has endured through the centuries. It dares to tackle the toughest questions about life: Where do I go after I die? Is there a God? What do I do with my fears? The Bible offers answers to these crucial questions. It is the treasure map that leads us to God's highest treasure, eternal life.

But how do we use the Bible? Countless copies of Scripture sit unread on bookshelves and nightstands simply because people don't know how to read it. What can we do to make the Bible real in our lives?

The clearest answer is found in the words of Jesus. He promised:

Ask, and God will give to you. Search, and you will find. Knock, and the door will open for you. (Matt. 7:7 NCV)

The first step in understanding the Bible is asking God to help us. We should read prayerfully. If anyone understands God's Word, it is because of God and not the reader.

But the Helper will teach you everything and will cause you to remember all that I told you. The Helper is the Holy Spirit whom the Father will send in my name. (John 14:26 NCV)

Before reading the Bible, pray. Invite God to speak to you. Don't go to Scripture looking for your idea; go searching for his.

Not only should we read the Bible prayerfully; we should read it carefully. *Search and you will find* is the pledge. The Bible is not a newspaper to be skimmed but rather a mine to be quarried.

Search for it like silver, and hunt for it like hidden treasure. Then you will understand respect for the LORD, and you will find that you know God. (Prov. 2:4–5 NCV)

Any worthy find requires effort. The Bible is no exception. To understand the Bible you don't have to be brilliant, but you must be willing to roll up your sleeves and search.

Be a worker who is not ashamed and who uses the true teaching in the right way. (2 Tim. 2:15 NCV)

Here's a practical point. Study the Bible a bit at a time. Hunger is not satisfied by eating twenty-one meals in one sitting once a week. The body needs a steady diet to remain strong. So does the soul. When God sent food to his people in the wilderness, he didn't provide loaves already made. Instead, he sent them manna in the shape of *"thin flakes like frost . . . on the desert ground"* (Ex. 16:14 NCV).

God gave manna in limited portions. God sends spiritual food the same way. He opens the heavens with just enough nutrients for today's hunger. He provides *"a command here, a command there. A rule here, a rule there. A little lesson here, a little lesson there"* (Isa. 28:10 NCV).

Don't be discouraged if your reading reaps a small harvest. Some days a lesser portion is all that is needed. What is important is to search every day for that day's message. A steady diet of God's Word over a lifetime builds a healthy soul and mind.

A little girl returned from her first day at school. Her mom asked, "Did you learn anything?"

"Apparently not enough," the girl responded, "I have to go back tomorrow and the next day and the next . . ."

Such is the case with learning. And such is the case with Bible study. Understanding comes little by little over a lifetime.

There is a third step in understanding the Bible. After the asking and seeking comes the knocking. After you ask and search, then knock.

Knock, and the door will open for you. (Matt. 7:7 NCV)

To knock is to stand at God's door. To make yourself available. To climb the steps, cross the porch, stand at the doorway, and volunteer. Knocking goes beyond the realm of thinking and into the realm of acting.

To knock is to ask, What can I do? How can I obey? Where can I go?

It's one thing to know what to do. It's another to do it. But for those who do it, those who choose to obey, a special reward awaits them.

The truly happy are those who carefully study God's perfect law that makes people free, and they continue to study it. They do not forget what they heard, but they obey what God's teaching says. Those who do this will be made happy. (James 1:25 NCV)

What a promise. Happiness comes to those who do what they read! It's the same with medicine. If you only read the label but ignore the pills, it won't help. It's the same with food. If you only read the recipe but never cook, you won't be fed. And it's the same with the Bible. If you only read the words but never obey, you'll never know the joy God has promised.

Ask. Search. Knock. Simple, isn't it? Why don't you give it a try? If you do, you'll see why you are holding the most remarkable book in history.

INTRODUCTION TO THE BOOK OF 1 THESSALONIANS

In the third century, Saint Cyprian wrote to a friend named Donatus:

> This seems a cheerful world, Donatus, when I view it from this fair garden under the shadow of these vines. But if I climbed some great mountain and looked out over the wide lands, you know very well what I would see: brigands on the high road, pirates on the seas, in the amphitheaters men murdered to please the applauding crowds, under all roofs misery and selfishness. It really is a bad world, Donatus, an incredibly bad world.
>
> Yet in the midst of it, I have found a quiet and holy people. They have discovered a joy which is a thousand times better than any pleasure of this sinful life. They are despised and persecuted, but they care not. They have overcome the world. These people are Christians . . . and I am one of them. (Gordon MacDonald, *Forging a Real-World Faith*)

What a compliment! *A quiet and holy people.* Is there any phrase that captures the essence of the faith any better? *A quiet and holy people.*

Quiet.

Not obnoxious. Not boastful. Not demanding. Just quiet. Contagiously quiet.

Holy.

Set apart. Pure. Decent. Honest. Wholesome. Holy. A quiet and holy people.

Paul urges the same from us.

"Do all you can to live a peaceful life. Take care of your own business, and do your own work as we have already told you. If you do, then people who are not believers will respect you, and you will not have to depend on others for what you need" (4:11–12 NCV).

A quiet and holy people. That describes the church in Thessalonica. May that describe the church today.

LESSON ONE

TRUE
TRANSFORMATION

MAX
LUCADO

REFLECTION

It's been said that the only two certainties in life are death and taxes. But we could add another item to that list—change. Think about it. Nothing in this world stays the same. Emotions vacillate. Relationships fluctuate. Material things deteriorate. Look at your own life and record some of the primary things that are different from ten years ago.

SITUATION

Paul and Silas were led by God to proclaim the good news of Christ's love in Thessalonica (see Acts 17:1–9). Many responded enthusiastically. However, when persecution forced these missionaries to depart abruptly, Paul wrote at the first opportunity. His intent? To commend the Thessalonians for their faith and to encourage them to continue to show and tell the gospel.

OBSERVATION

Read 1 Thessalonians 1:1–10 from the NCV or the NKJV.

NCV

¹From Paul, Silas, and Timothy.

To the church in Thessalonica, the church in God the Father and the Lord Jesus Christ:

Grace and peace to you.

²We always thank God for all of you and mention you when we pray. ³We continually recall before God our Father the things you have done because of your faith and the work you have done because of your love. And we thank him that you continue to be strong because of your hope in our Lord Jesus Christ.

⁴Brothers and sisters, God loves you, and we know he has chosen you, ⁵because the Good News we brought to you came not only with words, but with power, with the Holy Spirit, and with sure knowledge that it is true. Also you know how we lived when we were with you in order to help you. ⁶And you became like us and like the Lord. You suffered much, but still you accepted the teaching with the joy that comes from the Holy Spirit. ⁷So you became an example to all the believers in Macedonia and Southern Greece. ⁸And the Lord's teaching spread from you not only into Macedonia and Southern Greece, but now your faith in God has become known everywhere. So we do not need to say anything about it. ⁹People everywhere are telling about the way you accepted us when we were there with you. They tell how you stopped worshiping idols and began serving the living and true God. ¹⁰And you wait for God's Son, whom God raised from the dead, to come from heaven. He is Jesus, who saves us from God's angry judgment that is sure to come.

NKJV

¹Paul, Silvanus, and Timothy,

To the church of the Thessalonians in God the Father and the Lord Jesus Christ:

Grace to you and peace from God our Father and the Lord Jesus Christ. ²We give thanks to God always for you all, making mention of you in our prayers, ³remembering without ceasing your work of faith, labor of love, and patience of hope in our Lord Jesus Christ in the sight of our God and Father, ⁴knowing, beloved brethren, your election by God. ⁵For our gospel did not come to you in word only, but also in power, and in the Holy Spirit and in much assurance, as you know what kind of men we were among you for your sake.

⁶And you became followers of us and of the Lord, having received the word in much affliction, with joy of the Holy Spirit, ⁷so that you became examples to all in Macedonia and Achaia who believe. ⁸For from you the word of the Lord has sounded forth, not only in Macedonia and Achaia, but also in every place. Your faith toward God has gone out, so that we do not need to say anything. ⁹For they themselves declare concerning us what manner of entry we had to you, and how you turned to God from idols to serve the living and true God, ¹⁰and to wait for His Son from heaven, whom He raised from the dead, even Jesus who delivers us from the wrath to come.

EXPLORATION

1. Take three minutes to reread the history of the "founding" of the church at Thessalonica (Acts 17:1–9). How does their beginning compare with the history of your church?

2. What do Christians mean when they speak of "repenting" and "being converted"?

3. New Testament Christians seemed to face much more suffering and persecution than modern-day North American believers. Why?

4. What does it mean to present the good news "with power, with the Holy Spirit" (v. 5 NCV)?

5. Which is more important and why: a transformed character or a rock-solid reputation?

INSPIRATION

Here is (dare I say it?) the greatest miracle of God. It is astounding when God heals the body. It is extraordinary when God hears the prayer. It is incredible when God provides the new job, the new car, the new child. But none of these compares to when God creates new life.

At our new birth God remakes our souls and gives us what we need, again. New eyes so we can see by faith. A new mind so we can have the mind of Christ. New strength so we won't grow tired. A new vision so we won't lose heart. A new voice for praise and new hands for service. And most of all, a new heart. A heart that has been cleansed by Christ.

And, oh, how we need it. We have soiled what he gave us the first time. We have used our eyes to see impurity, our hands to give pain, our feet to walk the wrong path, our minds to think evil thoughts. All of us need to be made new again.

The first birth was for earthly life; the second one is for eternal life. The first time we received a physical heart; the second time we receive a spiritual heart. The first birth enabled us to have life on earth. The second birth enables us to have life eternal. (From *A Gentle Thunder* by Max Lucado)

REACTION

6. What were the circumstances surrounding your own conversion?

7. What prompted you to listen to the messengers who first explained the gospel to you?

8. What are the unmistakable signs that Christ has made you a new creature—that the Spirit of God lives in you?

9. In what specific ways do you feel that you are an example to other believers?

10. When others discuss your faith, what do you suspect they say about you, about God, about the church?

11. What areas of your life do you sense God's Spirit prompting you to look at?

LIFE LESSONS

Here's an arresting truth: You have a reputation. Good or bad, everyone who is acquainted with you has an opinion about you. If your name comes up in conversation, people think certain things. Good or bad, they remember specific interactions; they recall past incidents. If you are not around, they may say things about you. Do you know what they say? Good things? "She is one of the kindest people I know." Or bad things? "Oh, yeah, him . . . he's a self-absorbed jerk." The fact is, if we claim to be followers of Jesus, our reputation is enormously important. How do we go about making ours better? By working on our image? No. By focusing on our character. When we let God do his transforming work in our hearts, the difference Christ makes will slowly become evident on the surface of our lives.

DEVOTION

Father, thank you for the great hope of the gospel—that I don't have to stay like I am. I can change, by the power of your Spirit. Work in me. Show me the inconsistencies in my life. Help me to be a better example to those around me today.

For more Bible passages on our need to live transformed lives, see Daniel 1:8; Matthew 5:13–16; Acts 5:20; 1 Timothy 6:18; and 1 Peter 2:12; 3:15.

To complete the books of 1 and 2 Thessalonians during this twelve-part study, read 1 Thessalonians 1:1–10.

JOURNALING

We speak a lot about being changed by God. Yet how exactly does this transformation happen? What is God's part and what is our role?

LESSON TWO

THE
QUESTION
OF MOTIVES

MAX
LUCADO

REFLECTION

It isn't enough to merely do the right things. The Bible makes it clear that God cares not only about *what* we do, but *why* we do what we do. Take a few moments to honestly ponder your own heart in each of these areas:

Why do you go to church?

Why do you hang out with the friends you have chosen?

What are your motives for working where you do and the way you do?

SITUATION

After he left Thessalonica, the apostle Paul became the target of multiple false accusations—probably at the hands of pagan Gentiles who lived in the area, as well as the relentless band of hostile Jews who shadowed his movements. Here he writes to reveal his real motives for ministry.

OBSERVATION

Read 1 Thessalonians 2:1–12 from the NCV or the NKJV.

NCV

¹*Brothers and sisters, you know our visit to you was not a failure. ²Before we came to you, we suffered in Philippi. People there insulted us, as you know, and many people were against us. But our God helped us to be brave and to tell you his Good News. ³Our appeal does not come from lies or wrong reasons, nor were we trying to trick you. ⁴But we speak the Good News because God tested us and trusted us to do it. When we speak, we are not trying to please people, but God, who tests our hearts. ⁵You know that we never tried to influence you by saying nice things about you. We were not trying to get your money; we had no selfishness to hide from you. God knows that this is true. ⁶We were not looking for human praise, from you or anyone else, ⁷even though as apostles of Christ we could have used our authority over you.*

But we were very gentle with you, like a mother caring for her little children. ⁸Because we loved you, we were happy to share not only God's Good News with you, but even our own lives. You had become so dear to us! ⁹Brothers and sisters, I know you remember our hard work and difficulties. We worked night and day so we would not burden any of you while we preached God's Good News to you.

¹⁰*When we were with you, we lived in a holy and honest way, without fault. You know this is true, and so does God. ¹¹You know that we treated each of you as a father treats his own children. ¹²We encouraged you, we urged you, and we insisted that you live good lives for God, who calls you to his glorious kingdom.*

NKJV

¹*For you yourselves know, brethren, that our coming to you was not in vain. ²But even after we had suffered before and were spitefully treated at Philippi, as you know, we were bold in our God to speak to you the gospel of God in much conflict. ³For our exhortation did not come from error or uncleanness, nor was it in deceit.*

⁴*But as we have been approved by God to be entrusted with the gospel, even so we speak, not as pleasing men, but God who tests our hearts. ⁵For neither at any time did we use flattering words, as you know, nor a cloak for covetousness—God is witness. ⁶Nor did we seek glory from men, either from you or from others, when we might have made demands as apostles of Christ. ⁷But we were gentle among you, just as a nursing mother cherishes her own children. ⁸So, affectionately longing for you, we were well pleased to impart to you not only the gospel of God, but also our own lives, because you had become dear to us. ⁹For you remember, brethren, our labor and toil; for laboring night and day, that we might not be a burden to any of you, we preached to you the gospel of God.*

¹⁰*You are witnesses, and God also, how devoutly and justly and blamelessly we behaved ourselves among you who believe; ¹¹as you know how we exhorted, and comforted, and charged every one of you, as a father does his own children, ¹²that you would walk worthy of God who calls you into His own kingdom and glory.*

EXPLORATION

1. What is it like to have someone call your hard efforts a "failure" (see verse 1 NCV)?

2. Have you ever had the experience of having someone questioning your motives?

3. What is the advantage of being motivated by the one goal of trying to please God (v. 4 NCV)?

4. Look at Paul's various statements defending his motives and ministry. Can you echo those sentiments as you think back over your interactions with people from the last week?

5. What is Paul's point in using the analogies of motherhood (v. 7) and fatherhood (vv. 11–12)?

INSPIRATION

When I learned that [my Dad] had a terminal disease, I wrote him, volunteering to change my plans and stay near him. He immediately wrote back, saying, "Don't be concerned about me. I have no fear of death or eternity; just go . . . please him."

My father's life is an example of a heart melted in the fire of God, formed on his anvil, and used in his vineyard. He knew, and knows, what his life was for. In a society of question and confusion, his was one life that had a definition.

Time on God's anvil should do that for us: It should clarify our mission and define our purpose. When a tool emerges from a blacksmith's anvil, there is no question as to what it is for. There is no question as to why it was made. One look at the tool and you instantly know its function. You pick up a hammer and you know that it was made to hit nails. You pick up a saw and you know that it was made to cut wood. You see a screwdriver and you know that it is for tightening screws.

As a human being emerges from the anvil of God, the same should be true. Being tested by God reminds us that our function and task is to be about his business, that our purpose is to be an extension of his nature, an ambassador of his throne room, and a proclaimer of his message. We should exit the shop with no question as to why God made us. We know our purpose. (From *On the Anvil* by Max Lucado)

REACTION

6. How does having a clear sense of purpose or divine calling help us keep our motives pure in the daily hubbub of life?

7. How motivated are you by success and/or the fear of failure?

8. The temptation to be a people pleaser is powerful. How can a Christian realistically break free from this constant pressure?

9. Are our motives ever really 100 percent pure and noble?

10. Is conscience reliable? Can we let it be our guide in matters of motive?

11. What from Paul's transparent discussion of his motives stands out to you and challenges you to be different?

LIFE LESSONS

Someone has observed that we can choose to fear God, and if so, then we will fear nothing else. Or we can refuse to fear God—in which case, we will fear everything else. It is a powerful thing, a life-changing moment, when we realize that God's opinion is the only thing that ultimately matters. When we get to that place, we find true freedom. No more enslavement to the agendas of parents or peers. No more wringing our hands over what others think. We swap all those competing, confusing, crazy-making motivations for one simplified, bottom-line purpose: living to please God. We live our lives for an audience of one. Aren't you ready for such a life of simplicity and freedom, peace and power?

DEVOTION

Heavenly Father, thank you for the example of Paul. It is possible to be motivated purely by a love for you and a desire to honor you by serving others. That's what I want. Give me the grace to find that simple and free life.

For more Bible passages on motives, see Proverbs 16:7; John 8:29; 12:43; 2 Corinthians 5:9–10; Colossians 3:22; 1 Thessalonians 4:1; and Hebrews 11:5; 13:16.

To complete the books of 1 and 2 Thessalonians during this twelve-part study, read 1 Thessalonians 2:1–12.

JOURNALING

List any questionable motives in your life, and then, after writing 1 John 1:9 over the list, thank God for his promise to forgive and cleanse your heart.

WHEN HELL
BREAKS
LOOSE

MAX
LUCADO

REFLECTION

In his classic book *The Screwtape Letters*, the venerable C. S. Lewis warned of two possible errors in thinking about demons. On one extreme is the refusal to believe in their existence. The other equally dangerous mistake is to "feel an excessive and unhealthy interest in them." Which of these tendencies do you most see in your own life?

SITUATION

In this sobering passage, Paul reminds his readers that the world is immersed in a cosmic conflict. The "devil who rules this world" (2 Cor. 4:4 NCV) does not take lightly the spread of Christ's message. And he does not stand idly by when Christians seek to live to God's glory.

OBSERVATION

Read 1 Thessalonians 2:13–20 from the NCV or the NKJV.

NCV

¹³Also, we always thank God because when you heard his message from us, you accepted it as the word of God, not the words of humans. And it really is God's message which works in you who believe. ¹⁴Brothers and sisters, your experiences have been like those of God's churches in Christ that are in Judea. You suffered from the people of your own country, as they suffered from the Jews, ¹⁵who killed both the Lord Jesus and the prophets and forced us to leave that country. They do not please God and are against all people. ¹⁶They try to stop us from teaching those who are not Jews so they may be saved. By doing this, they are increasing their sins to the limit. The anger of God has come to them at last.

¹⁷Brothers and sisters, though we were separated from you for a short time, our thoughts were still with you. We wanted very much to see you and tried hard to do so. ¹⁸We wanted to come to you. I, Paul, tried to come more than once, but Satan stopped us. ¹⁹You are our hope, our joy, and the crown we will take pride in when our Lord Jesus Christ comes. ²⁰Truly you are our glory and our joy.

NKJV

¹³For this reason we also thank God without ceasing, because when you received the word of God which you heard from us, you welcomed it not as the word of men, but as it is in truth, the word of God, which also effectively works in you who believe. ¹⁴For you, brethren, became imitators of the churches of God which are in Judea in Christ Jesus. For you also suffered the same things from your own countrymen, just as they did from the Judeans, ¹⁵who killed both the Lord Jesus and their own prophets, and have persecuted us; and they do not please God and are contrary to all men, ¹⁶forbidding us to speak to the Gentiles that they may be saved, so as always to fill up the measure of their sins; but wrath has come upon them to the uttermost.

¹⁷But we, brethren, having been taken away from you for a short time in presence, not in heart, endeavored more eagerly to see your face with great desire. ¹⁸Therefore we wanted to come to you—even I, Paul, time and again—but Satan hindered us. ¹⁹For what is our hope, or joy, or crown of rejoicing? Is it not even you in the presence of our Lord Jesus Christ at His coming? ²⁰For you are our glory and joy.

EXPLORATION

1. What exactly does Paul mean when he says that *"God's message . . . works in you"* (v. 13 NCV)?

2. In your life as a believer, when have you encountered the most opposition?

3. The great antagonism and hostility to the Christian gospel that we see here (vv. 14–16, 18) and in church history—how do we explain this?

4. Explain Paul's relentless "obsession" to be with the Thessalonian believers (vv. 17–20).

5. In verse 18 Paul blames Satan for preventing him from returning to Thessalonica. How can we know when negative events are diabolical in nature and when they are just the result of living in a fallen world?

INSPIRATION

If God is for us, who can be against us? (Rom. 8:31 NIV) . . .

Indulge me for a moment. Four words in this verse deserve your attention. Read slowly the phrase "God is for us." Please pause for a minute before you continue. Read it again, aloud. (My apologies to the person next to you.) God is for us. Repeat the phrase four times, this time emphasizing each word. (Come on, you're not in that big of a hurry.)

God is for us.

God *is* for us.

God is *for* us.

God is for *us*.

God is for you. Your parents may have forgotten you, your teachers may have neglected you, your siblings may be ashamed of you, but within reach of your prayers is the Maker of the oceans. God!

God *is* for you. Not "may be," not "has been," not "was," not "would be," but "God is!" He is for you. Today. At this hour. At this minute. As you read this sentence. No need to wait in line or come back tomorrow. He is with you. He could not be closer than he is at this second. His loyalty won't increase if you are better nor lessen if you are worse. He is for you.

God is *for* you. Turn to the sidelines; that's God cheering your run. Look past the finish line; that's God applauding your steps. Listen for him in the bleachers, shouting your name. Too tired to continue? He'll carry you. Too discouraged to fight? He's picking you up. God is for you.

God is for *you*. Had he a calendar, your birthday would be circled. If he drove a car, your name would be on his bumper. If there's a tree in heaven, he's carved your name in the bark. We know he has a tattoo, and we know what it says. *"I have written your name on my hand,"* he declares (Isa. 49:16 NCV) . . .

God is with you. Knowing that, who is against you? Can death harm you now? Can disease rob your life? Can your purpose be taken or your value diminished? No. Though hell itself may set itself against you, no one can defeat you. You are protected. God is with you. (From *America Looks Up* by Max Lucado)

REACTION

6. When is it hardest for you to believe that God is for you?

7. What are your biggest struggles right now?

8. What are some of the more effective tools used by the enemy to keep the gospel from spreading, the church from prospering, and Christians from growing?

9. Paul mentions how his plans were hindered by Satan. Have you ever felt like this?

10. Paul expresses his deep desire to come and comfort the beleaguered Thessalonians. Who in your life is embroiled in a great spiritual struggle?

11. How would you finish this sentence: "My hope, joy, and the crown I will take pride in when Jesus comes is . . ."?

LIFE LESSONS

What happens when we get credible evidence of an impending terrorist attack? Everyone goes on high alert. In every possible way, we ratchet up the level of security. We become wary and vigilant. We take special precautions. We do all these things and more, because the failure to do them could and likely would be catastrophic. The same is true in the spiritual realm. We have a despicable, sworn enemy. Satan has declared all-out war on Christ and his church. While the outcome of this cosmic conflict is not in doubt, careless believers can still become casualties of the evil one. Our only hope? To hide ourselves in the God who loves us.

DEVOTION

O God, make me vigilant today. Remind me that life is war, that I am in the midst of a great cosmic struggle, and that I have an enemy who wants to destroy me. Protect me with your armor. Arm me with your wisdom and strength.

For more Bible passages on spiritual warfare, see Romans 7:23; 2 Corinthians 10:3–5; Ephesians 6:10–19; 1 Thessalonians 5:8; 1 Timothy 1:18; 6:12; 2 Timothy 2:4; and Hebrews 4:12.

To complete the books of 1 and 2 Thessalonians during this twelve-part study, read 1 Thessalonians 2:13–20.

JOURNALING

How would you convince a skeptical friend about the reality of Satan?

LESSON FOUR

ENCOURAGEMENT

MAX
LUCADO

REFLECTION

Possessions are nice. Abilities are great. But relationships are paramount. Can you imagine life without your friends and loved ones? Facing good times and bad without mentors and companions, fellow strugglers and wise counselors? Take a few minutes to list the ten people or families you'd love to have as neighbors in your "dream cul-de-sac."

SITUATION

Demonstrating his pastor's heart, the apostle Paul writes to the new Christians in Thessalonica to challenge them to stay strong in the faith. In this section of the letter, we get a reminder of how much believers need one another, as well as a few lessons in what it looks like to live a life of encouragement.

OBSERVATION

Read 1 Thessalonians 3:1–13 from the NCV or the NKJV.

NCV

¹When we could not wait any longer, we decided it was best to stay in Athens alone ²and send Timothy to you. Timothy, our brother, works with us for God and helps us tell people the Good News about Christ. We sent him to strengthen and encourage you in your faith ³so none of you would be upset by these troubles. You yourselves know that we must face these troubles. ⁴Even when we were with you, we told you we all would have to suffer, and you know it has happened. ⁵Because of this, when I could wait no longer, I sent Timothy to you so I could learn about your faith. I was afraid the devil had tempted you, and then our hard work would have been wasted.

6But Timothy now has come back to us from you and has brought us good news about your faith and love. He told us that you always remember us in a good way and that you want to see us just as much as we want to see you. 7So, brothers and sisters, while we have much trouble and suffering, we are encouraged about you because of your faith. 8Our life is really full if you stand strong in the Lord. 9We have so much joy before our God because of you. We cannot thank him enough for all the joy we feel. 10Night and day we continue praying with all our heart that we can see you again and give you all the things you need to make your faith strong.

11Now may our God and Father himself and our Lord Jesus prepare the way for us to come to you. 12May the Lord make your love grow more and multiply for each other and for all people so that you will love others as we love you. 13May your hearts be made strong so that you will be holy and without fault before our God and Father when our Lord Jesus comes with all his holy ones.

NKJV

1Therefore, when we could no longer endure it, we thought it good to be left in Athens alone, 2and sent Timothy, our brother and minister of God, and our fellow laborer in the gospel of Christ, to establish you and encourage you concerning your faith, 3that no one should be shaken by these afflictions; for you yourselves know that we are appointed to this. 4For, in fact, we told you before when we were with you that we would suffer tribulation, just as it happened, and you know. 5For this reason, when I could no longer endure it, I sent to know your faith, lest by some means the tempter had tempted you, and our labor might be in vain.

6But now that Timothy has come to us from you, and brought us good news of your faith and love, and that you always have good remembrance of us, greatly desiring to see us, as we also to see you— 7therefore, brethren, in all our affliction and distress we were comforted concerning you by your faith. 8For now we live, if you stand fast in the Lord.

9For what thanks can we render to God for you, for all the joy with which we rejoice for your sake before our God, 10night and day praying exceedingly that we may see your face and perfect what is lacking in your faith?

11Now may our God and Father Himself, and our Lord Jesus Christ, direct our way to you. 12And may the Lord make you increase and abound in love to one another and to all, just as we do to you, 13so that He may establish your hearts blameless in holiness before our God and Father at the coming of our Lord Jesus Christ with all His saints.

EXPLORATION

1. Comment on the interesting statement found in verse 2—that Timothy "works . . . for God" (NCV). What does that mean?

2. What are some concrete ideas for strengthening and encouraging others (see verse 2) in the faith?

3. If suffering is such a natural fact of life (see verses 3–4), why do we act so shocked when hard times come our way?

4. How would you finish the sentence in verse 8, answering honestly: "For now we live, if . . ." (NKJV)?

5. Who are the "Pauls and Timothys" in your life—the people who pray for you and exhort you and encourage you?

INSPIRATION

Had golf existed in the New Testament era, I'm sure the writers would have spoken of mulligans and foot wedges, but it didn't, so they wrote about running. The word *race* is from the Greek *agon,* from which we get the word *agony.* The Christian's race is not a jog but rather a demanding and grueling, sometimes agonizing race. It takes a massive effort to finish strong.

Likely you've noticed that many don't? Surely you've observed there are many on the side of the trail? They used to be running. There was a time when they kept the pace. But then weariness set in. They didn't think the run would be this tough. Or they were discouraged by a bump and daunted by a fellow runner. Whatever the reason, they don't run anymore. They may be Christians. They may come to church. They may put a buck in the plate and warm a pew, but their hearts aren't in the race. They retired before their time. Unless something changes, their best work will have been their first work, and they will finish with a whimper.

By contrast, Jesus' best work was his final work, and his strongest step was his last step. Our Master is the classic example of one who endured. The writer of Hebrews goes on to say that Jesus *"held on while wicked people were doing evil things to him"* (Heb. 12:3 NCV). The Bible says Jesus "held on," implying that Jesus could have "let go." The runner could have given up, sat down, gone home. He could have quit the race. But he didn't. "He held on while wicked people were doing evil things to him." (From *Just Like Jesus* by Max Lucado)

REACTION

6. Why is it important to run the race of the Christian life *alongside other runners?*

7. Paul obviously considered Timothy extremely reliable. How does a person develop this quality of dependability?

8. Why is it important to invest your life in other people (and not just in projects)?

9. Do you think, when your spiritual leaders reflect on your life, growth, influence, etc., that they are encouraged or discouraged? Why?

10. What are your biggest struggles right now?

11. It's been said, "Everybody needs a spiritual mentor, and everybody needs to mentor someone else." In your life, who fills the roles of the person you mentor and the person who mentors you?

LIFE LESSONS

How easy it is to forget that people are what matter. It's relationships that count. God calls us to a life in community. We are to grow together. We are to serve and minister together. This is the genius of the Christian faith. As we are guided by God's truth, empowered by God's Spirit, and surrounded by God's people, then and only then are we able to finish the race. We need the encouragement of older and wiser saints. We need to be encouraging those new believers that God is calling to himself. Are you part of a healthy body of believers? Are you committed to doing life together with a band of brothers and sisters? Ask God for a mentor. Ask God to give you somebody to mentor.

DEVOTION

Father, Son, and Holy Spirit, keep me from the grave error of thinking that I can live the Christian life on my own. I need the encouragement of other believers, and they need to be built up by the gifts that you have given me. May I move closer to others today.

For more Bible passages on encouraging others, see Acts 4:36; 15:32; Romans 12:8; Ephesians 6:22; Philippians 2:1; Colossians 4:8; Philemon 1:7; and Hebrews 3:13; 10:25.

To complete the books of 1 and 2 Thessalonians during this twelve-part study, read 1 Thessalonians 3:1–13.

JOURNALING

Instead of writing in your journal, take a few minutes to write an e-mail or note of appreciation to someone who has been used by God to encourage you spiritually.

PERSONAL PURITY

MAX
LUCADO

REFLECTION

Sex. It's probably *the* single most thought-about and talked about subject on earth. It's also probably the one area where people experience the most disappointment and heartache. Many Christians and churches are often reluctant to discuss this issue (except perhaps with their teens, and then usually only in a youth group setting). How many sermons on biblical sexuality have you heard at your church?

SITUATION

Paul counseled the fledgling church at Thessalonica to stand up and stand out for Christ by remaining sexually pure in the midst of an immoral culture.

OBSERVATION

Read 1 Thessalonians 4:1–12 from the NCV or the NKJV.

NCV

¹Brothers and sisters, we taught you how to live in a way that will please God, and you are living that way. Now we ask and encourage you in the Lord Jesus to live that way even more. ²You know what we told you to do by the authority of the Lord Jesus. ³God wants you to be holy and to stay away from sexual sins. ⁴He wants each of you to learn to control your own body in a way that is holy and honorable. ⁵Don't use your body for sexual sin like the people who do not know God. ⁶Also, do not wrong or cheat another Christian in this way. The Lord will punish people who do those things as we have already told you and warned you. ⁷God called us to be holy and does not want us to live in sin. ⁸So the person who refuses to obey this teaching is disobeying God, not simply a human teaching. And God is the One who gives us his Holy Spirit.

⁹We do not need to write you about having love for your Christian family, because God has already taught you to love each other. ¹⁰And truly you do love the Christians in all of Macedonia. Brothers and sisters, now we encourage you to love them even more.

¹¹Do all you can to live a peaceful life. Take care of your own business, and do your own work as we have already told you. ¹²If you do, then people who are not believers will respect you, and you will not have to depend on others for what you need.

NKJV

¹Finally then, brethren, we urge and exhort in the Lord Jesus that you should abound more and more, just as you received from us how you ought to walk and to please God; ²for you know what commandments we gave you through the Lord Jesus.

³For this is the will of God, your sanctification: that you should abstain from sexual immorality; ⁴that each of you should know how to possess his own vessel in sanctification and honor, ⁵not in passion of lust, like the Gentiles who do not know God; ⁶that no one should take advantage of and defraud his brother in this matter, because the Lord is the avenger of all such, as we also forewarned you and testified. ⁷For God did not call us to uncleanness, but in holiness. ⁸Therefore he who rejects this does not reject man, but God, who has also given us His Holy Spirit.

⁹But concerning brotherly love you have no need that I should write to you, for you yourselves are taught by God to love one another; ¹⁰and indeed you do so toward all the brethren who are in all Macedonia. But we urge you, brethren, that you increase more and more; ¹¹that you also aspire to lead a quiet life, to mind your own business, and to work with your own hands, as we commanded you, ¹²that you may walk properly toward those who are outside, and that you may lack nothing.

EXPLORATION

1. What constitutes "sexual immorality" (v. 3 NKJV)?

2. Why do you think sexual temptation is so powerful?

3. How do you think God views sex?

4. Summarize Paul's counsel to the Thessalonians on matters of sex.

5. How, practically and realistically, does a Christian learn to control his or her own body in pure ways (v. 4 NCV)?

INSPIRATION

You're acquainted with house-sitters. You've possibly used one. Not wanting to leave your house vacant, you ask someone to stay in your home until you return. Let me describe two of your nightmares.

The house-sitter redecorates your house. White paint is changed to pink. Berber carpet to shag. An abstract plastic chair sits in the place of your cozy love seat. His justification? "The house didn't express me accurately. I needed a house that communicated who I am."

Your response? "It's not yours! My residence does not exist to reflect you! I asked you to take care of the house, not take over the house!" Would you want a sitter like this?

You might choose him over nightmare number two. She didn't redecorate; she neglected. Never washed a dish, made a bed, or took out the trash. "My time here was temporary. I knew you wouldn't mind," she explains.

Of course you'd mind! Does she know what this abode cost you?

Both house-sitters made the same mistake. They acted as if the dwelling were theirs. How could they?

Or, better asked, how could we? When it comes to our bodies, the Bible declares that we don't own them. *"You are no longer your own. God paid a great price for you. So use your body to honor God"* (1 Cor. 6:19–20 CEV).

Use your body to indulge your passions? To grab attention? To express your opinions? No. Use your body to honor God. *"Use your whole body as a tool to do what is right for the glory of God"* (Rom. 6:13 NLT). Your body is God's instrument, intended for his work and for his glory. (From *It's Not About Me* by Max Lucado)

REACTION

6. How would your sexual thoughts and habits change if you were able to deeply grasp the truth that God owns and lives in your body?

7. The principle in verse 1 is "You're doing good—now do even better." In what areas of your life are you moving in a positive direction?

8. How would you explain holiness to an eight-year-old?

9. What counsel would you give to someone with a strong temptation to have an affair, or to someone addicted to pornography?

10. What constitutes sexual addiction?

11. At the end of this passage, Paul stresses love (as opposed to sex) and living a purposeful life. How can these emphases help one develop healthy attitudes and habits in the area of sex?

LIFE LESSONS

Sexual purity is important because sex—like everything else—was created by God and for his glory (see Colossians 1:16). It's crucial to remember that God is *for* sex. He made physical intimacy to be wondrous and pleasurable. He decreed sexual union to be good, when reserved for marriage between a man and woman. He established the sexual act to serve as a physical illustration of the spiritual intimacy and passion creatures can have in knowing their Creator (Eph. 5:22–33). Any abuse or misuse of this beautiful gift (premarital sex, adultery, rape, incest, sexual child abuse, pornography, lust, masturbation, homosexuality, bestiality, etc.) distorts the picture and robs God of the glory that he so richly deserves.

DEVOTION

Father, in a sex-saturated, lust-obsessed culture, grant me the wisdom to guard my eyes and my heart. Help me to see sex through your eyes—as beautiful and good. Help me to honor you in my body.

For more Bible passages on sexual purity, see Deuteronomy 5:18; Job 31:1; Proverbs 5:20; Matthew 5:28; 1 Corinthians 7:1; Colossians 3:5; Titus 2:5; Hebrews 13:4; and 1 Peter 2:11.

To complete the books of 1 and 2 Thessalonians during this twelve-part study, read 1 Thessalonians 4:1–12.

JOURNALING

What are some of the outside influences in your life that project a distorted view of sexuality?

THE KING IS COMING!

MAX LUCADO

REFLECTION

For centuries people have been fascinated and fixated on the end of the world. The Second Coming of Christ. Armageddon. Judgment. Many have even tried to predict when all these things will occur. What are your honest thoughts about this subject? Do you enjoy wondering and studying about the return of Christ?

SITUATION

Writing to a young congregation of believers he recently helped establish, the apostle Paul answers some of their questions (sent via Timothy) about the return of Christ.

OBSERVATION

Read 1 Thessalonians 4:13–5:11 from the NCV or the NKJV.

NCV

13Brothers and sisters, we want you to know about those Christians who have died so you will not be sad, as others who have no hope. 14We believe that Jesus died and that he rose again. So, because of him, God will raise with Jesus those who have died. 15What we tell you now is the Lord's own message. We who are living when the Lord comes again will not go before those who have already died. 16The Lord himself will come down from heaven with a loud command, with the voice of the archangel, and with the trumpet call of God. And those who have died believing in Christ will rise first. 17After that, we who are still alive will be gathered up with them in the clouds to meet the Lord in the air. And we will be with the Lord forever. 18So encourage each other with these words.

5:1Now, brothers and sisters, we do not need to write you about times and dates. 2You know very well that the day the Lord comes again will be a surprise, like a thief that comes in the night. 3While people are saying, "We have peace and we are safe," they will be destroyed quickly. It is like pains that come quickly to a woman having a baby. Those people will not escape. 4But you, brothers and sisters, are not living in darkness, and so that day will not surprise you like a thief. 5You are all people who belong to the light and to the day. We do not belong to the night or to darkness. 6So we should not be like other people who are sleeping, but we should be alert and have self-control. 7Those who sleep, sleep at night. Those who get drunk, get drunk at night. 8But we belong to the day, so we should control ourselves. We should wear faith and love to protect us, and the hope of salvation should be our helmet. 9God did not choose us to suffer his anger but to have salvation through our Lord Jesus Christ. 10Jesus died for us so that we can live together with him, whether we are alive or dead when he comes. 11So encourage each other and give each other strength, just as you are doing now.

NKJV

13But I do not want you to be ignorant, brethren, concerning those who have fallen asleep, lest you sorrow as others who have no hope. 14For if we believe that Jesus died and rose again, even so God will bring with Him those who sleep in Jesus.

15For this we say to you by the word of the Lord, that we who are alive and remain until the coming of the Lord will by no means precede those who are asleep. 16For the Lord Himself will descend from heaven with a shout, with the voice of an archangel, and with the trumpet of God. And the dead in Christ will rise first. 17Then we who are alive and remain shall be caught up together with them in the clouds to meet the Lord in the air. And thus we shall always be with the Lord. 18Therefore comfort one another with these words.

5:1But concerning the times and the seasons, brethren, you have no need that I should write to you. 2For you yourselves know perfectly that the day of the Lord so comes as a thief in the night. 3For when they say, "Peace and safety!" then sudden destruction comes upon them, as labor pains upon a pregnant woman. And they shall not escape. 4But you, brethren, are not in darkness, so that this Day should overtake you as a thief. 5You are all sons of light and sons of the day. We are not of the night nor of darkness. 6Therefore let us not sleep, as others do, but let us watch and be sober. 7For those who sleep, sleep at night, and those who get drunk are drunk at night. 8But let us who are of the day be sober, putting on the breastplate of faith and love, and as a helmet the hope of salvation. 9For God did not appoint us to wrath, but to obtain salvation through our Lord Jesus Christ, 10who died for us, that whether we wake or sleep, we should live together with Him.

11Therefore comfort each other and edify one another, just as you also are doing.

EXPLORATION

1. Why don't Christians have to be sad when one of our own dies?

2. What will happen to living Christians when Christ returns?

3. Paul meant for his words here to be an encouragement and a comfort. How do they make you feel?

4. When will all these end-time events transpire?

5. What practical difference should the return of Christ make in our lives?

INSPIRATION

Listen in on any discussion about the return of Christ, and someone will inquire, "But what about those who have already died? What happens to Christians between their death and Jesus' return?"

Apparently the church in Thessalonica asked such a question. Listen to Paul's words to them: *"We want you to be quite certain, brothers, about those who have died, to make sure that you do not grieve about them, like the other people who have no hope"* (1 Thess. 4:13 TJB).

The Thessalonian church had buried her share of loved ones. And Paul wants the members who remain to be at peace regarding the ones who have gone ahead. Many of you have buried loved ones as well. And just as God spoke to them, he speaks to you.

If you'll celebrate a marriage anniversary alone this year, he speaks to you.

If your child made it to heaven before making it to kindergarten, he speaks to you.

If you lost a loved one in violence, if you learned more than you want to know about disease, if your dreams were buried as they lowered the casket, God speaks to you.

He speaks to all of us who have stood or will stand in the soft dirt near an open grave. And to us he gives this confident word: *"I want you to know what happens to a Christian when he dies so that when it happens, you will not be full of sorrow, as those are who have no hope. For since we believe that Jesus died and then came back to life again, we can also believe that when Jesus returns, God will bring back with him all the Christians who have died"* (1 Thess. 4:13–14 TLB).

God transforms our hopeless grief into hope-filled grief. How? By telling us that we will see our loved ones again. (From *When Christ Comes* by Max Lucado)

REACTION

6. What believing friends or loved ones have you lost?

7. What questions or emotions rise up in you when you read 4:16–17?

8. Even though nobody knows when Christ will return, do you sometimes sense it will be in your lifetime? Why?

9. What did Paul mean when he said that we *"belong to the light and to the day. We do not belong to the night or to darkness"* (5:5 NCV)?

10. Why does Paul mention the *"breastplate of faith"* and the *"helmet . . . of salvation"* (5:8 NKJV)? What's his point?

11. How could you use this section of Scripture to help someone who is grieving the death of a loved one?

LIFE LESSONS

Have you ever wondered what that "loud command" of verse 16 (NCV) will be? It will be the first audible message most have heard from God. It will be the word which closes one age and opens a new one. I could very well be wrong, but I think the command which puts an end to the sorrows of earth and initiates the joys of heaven for the people of God will be two words: "No more." Perhaps the King of kings will raise his pierced hand and proclaim, "No more." No more loneliness. No more tears. No more death. No more sadness. No more crying. No more pain. Jesus promised that "the end will come" (Matt. 24:14 NKJV). For those who live for this world, that's bad news. But for those who live for the world to come, it's an encouraging promise.

DEVOTION

Lord Jesus, come quickly! But whether your return is tomorrow or two hundred years from now, let me live in a way that honors you and that points others to you.

For more Bible passages on living in light of the sure return of Christ, see Matthew 24:27–51; 26:64; John 14:1–3; Acts 1:11; Philippians 3:20–21; 2 Timothy 4:1; Hebrews 9:28; 1 John 2:28; and Revelation 3:11.

To complete the books of 1 and 2 Thessalonians during this twelve-part study, read 1 Thessalonians 4:13–5:11.

JOURNALING

List five specific ways you would need to change your life to live out the truth in
1 John 2:28 and 1 Thessalonians 5:8.

THE
CHRISTIAN'S
SURVIVAL
KIT

MAX
LUCADO

REFLECTION

"Pride goes before a fall." "A penny saved is a penny earned." "It's possible to do something in a moment that you'll regret for a lifetime." We hear maxims and proverbs like these all the time. What wise sayings or concise bits of advice have had the biggest impact on *your* life?

SITUATION

Forced to leave Thessalonica before he had adequately instructed the new Christians there, Paul wrote this letter to teach and encourage this new church. In closing, he reminded them of some very basic, but very important truths for living as God's people.

OBSERVATION

Read 1 Thessalonians 5:12–28 from the NCV or the NKJV.

NCV

12Now, brothers and sisters, we ask you to appreciate those who work hard among you, who lead you in the Lord and teach you. 13Respect them with a very special love because of the work they do.

Live in peace with each other. 14We ask you, brothers and sisters, to warn those who do not work. Encourage the people who are afraid. Help those who are weak. Be patient with everyone. 15Be sure that no one pays back wrong for wrong, but always try to do what is good for each other and for all people.

16Always be joyful. 17Pray continually, 18and give thanks whatever happens. That is what God wants for you in Christ Jesus.

19Do not hold back the work of the Holy Spirit. 20Do not treat prophecy as if it were unimportant. 21But test everything. Keep what is good, 22and stay away from everything that is evil.

23Now may God himself, the God of peace, make you pure, belonging only to him. May your whole self—spirit, soul, and body—be kept safe and without fault when our Lord Jesus Christ comes. 24You can trust the One who calls you to do that for you.

²⁵*Brothers and sisters, pray for us.*

²⁶*Give each other a holy kiss when you meet.* ²⁷*I tell you by the authority of the Lord to read this letter to all the believers.*

²⁸*The grace of our Lord Jesus Christ be with you.*

NKJV

¹²*And we urge you, brethren, to recognize those who labor among you, and are over you in the Lord and admonish you,* ¹³*and to esteem them very highly in love for their work's sake. Be at peace among yourselves.*

¹⁴*Now we exhort you, brethren, warn those who are unruly, comfort the fainthearted, uphold the weak, be patient with all.* ¹⁵*See that no one renders evil for evil to anyone, but always pursue what is good both for yourselves and for all.*

¹⁶*Rejoice always,* ¹⁷*pray without ceasing,* ¹⁸*in everything give thanks; for this is the will of God in Christ Jesus for you.*

¹⁹*Do not quench the Spirit.* ²⁰*Do not despise prophecies.* ²¹*Test all things; hold fast what is good.* ²²*Abstain from every form of evil.*

²³*Now may the God of peace Himself sanctify you completely; and may your whole spirit, soul, and body be preserved blameless at the coming of our Lord Jesus Christ.* ²⁴*He who calls you is faithful, who also will do it.*

²⁵*Brethren, pray for us.*

²⁶*Greet all the brethren with a holy kiss.*

²⁷*I charge you by the Lord that this epistle be read to all the holy brethren.*

²⁸*The grace of our Lord Jesus Christ be with you. Amen.*

EXPLORATION

1. How should Christians view and respond to their spiritual leaders?

2. We know that living "in peace" with other Christians is a frequent Bible topic (v. 13 NCV). What makes this simple command so difficult to live out?

3. How is it possible to *always* be joyful?

4. What are some ways we "quench the Spirit" (v. 19 NKJV)?

5. Paul urges his readers to live pure lives, but then he concludes this letter by saying, *"Now may God himself . . . make you pure"* (v. 23 NCV). How are we pure—through ourselves or through God? Don't Paul's words sound like contradictions?

INSPIRATION

I'm an offspring of sturdy stock. A product of a rugged, blue-collar culture that honored decency, loyalty, hard work, and loved Bible verses like, "God helps those who help themselves." (No, it's not in there.)

"God started it and now we must finish it" was our motto. He's done his part; now we do ours. It's a fifty-fifty proposition. A do-it-yourself curriculum that majors in our part and minors in God's part.

"Blessed are the busy" this theology proclaims, "for they are the true Christians."

No need for the supernatural. No place for the extraordinary. No room for the transcendent . . .

It's a wind-the-world-up-and-walk-away view of God. And the philosophy works . . . as long as you work. Your faith is strong, as long as you are strong. Your position is secure, as long as you are secure. Your life is good, as long as you are good.

But, alas, therein lies the problem. As the Teacher said, *"No one is good"* (Matt. 19:17 NKJV). Nor is anyone always strong; nor is anyone always secure.

Do-it-yourself Christianity is not much encouragement to the done in and worn out.

Self-sanctification holds little hope for the addict.

"Try a little harder" is little encouragement for the abused.

At some point we need more than good advice; we need help. Somewhere on this journey home we realize that a fifty-fifty proposition is too little. We need more—more than a pudgy wizard who thanks us for coming but tells us the trip was unnecessary.

We need help. Help from the inside out. The kind of help Jesus promised. *"I will ask the Father, and he will give you another Helper to be with you forever—the Spirit of truth. The world cannot accept him, because it does not see him or know him. But you know him, because he lives with you and will be in you"* (John 14:16–17 NCV, emphasis mine).

Note the final words of the verse. And in doing so, note the dwelling place of God—"in you."

Not near us. Not above us. Not around us. But in us. In the part of us we don't even know. In the heart no one else has seen. In the hidden recesses of our being dwells, not an angel, not a philosophy, not a genie, but God.

Imagine that. (From *When God Whispers Your Name* by Max Lucado)

REACTION

6. How easy or hard is it for you to grasp the reality that God lives in you to strengthen you and guide you and transform you?

7. What are some specific ways you could show greater respect and love to your spiritual leaders?

8. On a scale of 1 to 10, with 1 being "hellish" and 10 being "heavenly," how peaceful are your closest relationships right now?

9. Describe what it looks like to "pray continually" (v. 17 NCV)?

10. How thankful are you? How can a person develop a more thankful attitude?

11. Which of these final instructions from Paul seems the most pertinent to your life just now?

LIFE LESSONS

Our culture worships at the altars of independence and autonomy. We like to fancy ourselves as "rugged individualists." It would be more accurate to describe us as disconnected and vulnerable. Under the foolish banner of self-sufficiency, millions face life daily without the healthy safeguard of community. The result is loneliness and lives that spin out of control. One of the big lessons of 1 Thessalonians (and the whole Bible, really) is that God made us to be interdependent. We really do need spiritual leaders and fellow strugglers. And others need our encouragement. Humans were never meant to fly solo. The traveler who ventures out alone has less joy than the one who journeys with some companions. The soldier who fights all by himself is an easy target for the enemy. Where's *your* community?

DEVOTION

Lord Jesus, thank you for spiritual leaders and for brothers and sisters in Christ. Help me grow stronger and deeper and wiser as I participate fully in a healthy community that is devoted to ministry.

For more Bible passages on living a strong and holy life, see 1 Corinthians 6:18; 1 Thessalonians 3:12; and 2 Thessalonians 3:10–12.

To complete the books of 1 and 2 Thessalonians during this twelve-part study, read 1 Thessalonians 5:12–28.

JOURNALING

Make a list of things that make you joyful.

INTRODUCTION TO THE BOOK OF 2 THESSALONIANS

I'm seated on an airplane. A grounded airplane. I'm surrounded by kids. Restless kids.

The kids are mine. The plane is not. The plane is late, however, and my kids are restless. I took them with me on a trip so we'd have a bit of time together. This is more than I had in mind.

They ask the questions you'd expect of a five- and eight-year-old. "Are they bringing drinks yet?"

"When are we going to leave?"

"How much more time?"

"Are we nearly home?"

"Why is it taking so long?"

Questions. Lots of questions. The kind of questions that were circulating through the church at Thessalonica. They, too, were restless. Somewhere they got the idea that Jesus was returning tomorrow, so they got ready. Some were selling their homes, others were quitting their work, and all were twiddling their thumbs while awaiting the return of Christ.

Paul gets wind of their assumption and writes them this letter. He urges them not to buy into the reports that the final days have already begun (2:1–2). Several things still need to occur first (2:3–12), and until they do, their task is to be patient and alert.

No easy task. Human nature tends to be one or the other. We tend to be so patient we aren't alert, or so alert we aren't patient. The church becomes the hybrid of the restless and the resting. The result can be squabbling kids. Just like mine. They've done their best to be patient, but after awhile a person can only take so much.

"Hang in there," I say.

"We'll be home soon," I urge.

"Try to get along," I exhort.

(I'm starting to sound a lot like Paul.)

THE UPSIDE
OF TROUBLE

MAX
LUCADO

REFLECTION

Some people wilt when hard times come; others seem to get stronger. Some believers become embittered when they encounter suffering, while others become more like Christ. How do we explain this phenomenon?

SITUATION

In his second letter to the Christians in Thessalonica, Paul expresses gratitude to God for their continued growth, and he exhorts them to remain faithful through times of persecution and suffering.

OBSERVATION

Read 2 Thessalonians 1:1–12 from the NCV or the NKJV.

NCV

¹From Paul, Silas, and Timothy.

To the church in Thessalonica in God our Father and the Lord Jesus Christ:

²Grace and peace to you from God the Father and the Lord Jesus Christ.

³We must always thank God for you, brothers and sisters. This is only right, because your faith is growing more and more, and the love that every one of you has for each other is increasing. ⁴So we brag about you to the other churches of God. We tell them about the way you continue to be strong and have faith even though you are being treated badly and are suffering many troubles.

⁵This is proof that God is right in his judgment. He wants you to be counted worthy of his kingdom for which you are suffering. ⁶God will do what is right. He will give trouble to those who trouble you. ⁷And he will give rest to you who are troubled and to us also when the Lord Jesus appears with burning fire from heaven with his powerful angels. ⁸Then he will punish those who do not know God and who do not obey the Good News about our Lord Jesus Christ. ⁹Those people will be punished with a destruction that continues forever. They will be kept away from the Lord and from his great power. ¹⁰This will happen on the day when the Lord Jesus comes to receive glory because of his holy people. And all the people who have believed will be amazed at Jesus. You will be in that group, because you believed what we told you.

¹¹That is why we always pray for you, asking our God to help you live the kind of life he called you to live. We pray that with his power God will help you do the good things you want and perform the works that come from your faith. ¹²We pray all this so that the name of our Lord Jesus Christ will have glory in you, and you will have glory in him. That glory comes from the grace of our God and the Lord Jesus Christ.

NKJV

¹Paul, Silvanus, and Timothy,

To the church of the Thessalonians in God our Father and the Lord Jesus Christ:

²Grace to you and peace from God our Father and the Lord Jesus Christ.

³We are bound to thank God always for you, brethren, as it is fitting, because your faith grows exceedingly, and the love of every one of you all abounds toward each other, ⁴so that we ourselves boast of you among the churches of God for your patience and faith in all your persecutions and tribulations that you endure, ⁵which is manifest evidence of the righteous judgment of God, that you may be counted worthy of the kingdom of God, for which you also suffer; ⁶since it is a righteous thing with God to repay with tribulation those who trouble you, ⁷and to give you who are troubled rest with us when the Lord Jesus is revealed from heaven with His mighty angels, ⁸in flaming fire taking vengeance on those who do not know God, and on those who do not obey the gospel of our Lord Jesus Christ. ⁹These shall be punished with everlasting destruction from the presence of the Lord and from the glory of His power, ¹⁰when He comes, in that Day, to be glorified in His saints and to be admired among all those who believe, because our testimony among you was believed.

¹¹Therefore we also pray always for you that our God would count you worthy of this calling, and fulfill all the good pleasure of His goodness and the work of faith with power, ¹²that the name of our Lord Jesus Christ may be glorified in you, and you in Him, according to the grace of our God and the Lord Jesus Christ.

EXPLORATION

1. Paul begins his letter by praising the Thessalonians. If your pastor were talking to a fellow minister about you and your church, what specific things would he brag about?

2. Are you shocked when God allows you to go through really painful experiences?

3. What is your "theology of suffering"? In other words, how do you reconcile bad things with a good and powerful God?

4. Have you ever been persecuted because of your faith?

5. Put yourself in the place of the Thessalonians. How would these verses, these assurances of prayer, have encouraged you?

INSPIRATION

"My thoughts are not like your thoughts. Your ways are not like my ways. Just as the heavens are higher than the earth, so are my ways higher than your ways and my thoughts higher than your thoughts" (Isa. 55:8–9 NCV).

Make special note of the word *like*. God's thoughts are not our thoughts, nor are they even *like* ours. We aren't even in the same neighborhood. We're thinking, *Preserve the body;* he's thinking, *Save the soul.* We dream of a pay raise. He dreams of raising the dead. We avoid pain and seek peace. God uses pain to bring peace. "I'm going to live before I die," we resolve. "Die so you can live," he instructs. We love what rusts. He loves what endures. We rejoice at our successes. He rejoices at our confessions. We show our children the Nike star with the million-dollar smile and say, "Be like Mike." God points to the crucified carpenter with bloody lips and a torn side and says, "Be like Christ."

Our thoughts are not like God's thoughts. Our ways are not like his ways. He has a different agenda. He dwells in a different dimension. He lives on another plan . . .

How vital that we pray, armed with the knowledge that God is in heaven. Pray with any lesser conviction, and our prayers are timid, shallow, and hollow. Look up and see what God has done, and watch how your prayers are energized.

This knowledge gives us confidence as we face the uncertain future. We know that he is in control of the universe, and so we can rest secure. But important also is the knowledge that this God in heaven has chosen to bend near toward earth to see our sorrow and hear our prayers. He is not so far above us that he is not touched by our tears.

Though we may not be able to see his purpose or his plan, the Lord of heaven is on his throne and in firm control of the universe and our lives. So we entrust him with our future. We entrust him with our very lives. (From *America Looks Up* by Max Lucado)

REACTION

6. Which is worse—the suffering that comes to all men because of disasters, death, etc., or the suffering that comes from being persecuted for one's faith?

7. How can God possibly be glorified through the suffering of his saints? Wouldn't he get more glory out of dramatically rescuing them?

8. When facing severe trials, how, realistically and specifically, can a Christian keep the faith?

9. Does prayer really make a difference in the lives of those who are suffering? How?

10. How does the biblical assurance of God's ultimate justice help make sense of persecution?

11. Should a Christian be concerned if he or she has never been the recipient of persecution? Why or why not?

LIFE LESSONS

"Everyone who wants to live as God desires, in Christ Jesus, will be hurt" (2 Tim. 3:12 NCV). Some promise, huh? Not the kind of Bible verse we tend to commit to memory—or to needlepoint, and then frame and hang about the living room sofa! And yet it *is* a divine guarantee. So, what do we do with such a sobering statement? A few suggestions . . . We use it to remind ourselves that this world is not our home. We use it to increase our longing for the Lord's return. We trust that behind such a stark statement stands a God who is always faithful, infinitely powerful, and perfectly good. Whatever we need in times of trial—help, hope, strength—he pledges to supply. His grace is always sufficient. And the next world's rewards to those who persevere through this world's difficulties will far exceed our wildest dreams.

DEVOTION

Father, I don't understand suffering, and I am not eager to face persecution. But if and when those things come, I trust that you are in control and that you are good. All I need I find in you.

For more Bible passages on suffering, see Matthew 5:11; 10:22, 39; Acts 5:30–31; Romans 8:17; 2 Corinthians 4:11; Hebrews 11:25; James 5:10; and 1 Peter 2:20; 5:10.

To complete the books of 1 and 2 Thessalonians during this twelve-part study, read 2 Thessalonians 1:1–12.

JOURNALING

It's been reported that more Christians suffered and died for their faith in the twentieth century than in the previous nineteen centuries combined. Why, do you think? How do we explain this apparent spike in persecution?

THE GREAT DECEIVER

MAX LUCADO

REFLECTION

No doubt you've seen that common cartoon character—the somber, bearded man in a white robe, holding a sign that says "Repent! The End Is Near!" Maybe you've even run across such a person in real life. What's your reaction when preachers or Christians start talking about the "end times"? About the devil? About hell?

SITUATION

Wrongly believing the claims made by certain false teachers that the "day of the Lord" had arrived, some of the Christians in Thessalonica had quit their jobs and were waiting for Christ to rescue them from persecution. Paul addressed this erroneous theological thinking, urging the believers to live responsibly and resolutely.

OBSERVATION

Read 2 Thessalonians 2:1–12 from the NCV or the NKJV.

NCV

¹Brothers and sisters, we have something to say about the coming of our Lord Jesus Christ and the time when we will meet together with him. ²Do not become easily upset in your thinking or afraid if you hear that the day of the Lord has already come. Someone may say this in a prophecy or in a message or in a letter as if it came from us. ³Do not let anyone fool you in any way. That day of the Lord will not come until the turning away from God happens and the Man of Evil, who is on his way to hell, appears. ⁴He will be against and put himself above anything called God or anything that people worship. And that Man of Evil will even go into God's Temple and sit there and say that he is God.

⁵I told you when I was with you that all this would happen. Do you not remember? ⁶And now you know what is stopping that Man of Evil so he will appear at the right time. ⁷The secret power of evil is already working in the world, but there is one who is stopping that power. And he will continue to stop it until he is taken out of the way. ⁸Then that Man of Evil will appear, and the Lord Jesus will kill him with the breath that comes from his mouth and will destroy him with the glory of his coming. ⁹The Man of Evil will come by the power of Satan. He will have great power, and he will do many different false miracles, signs, and wonders. ¹⁰He will use every kind of evil to trick those who are lost. They will die, because they refused to love the truth. (If they loved the truth, they would be saved.) ¹¹For this reason God sends them something powerful that leads them away from the truth so they will believe a lie. ¹²So all those will be judged guilty who did not believe the truth, but enjoyed doing evil.

NKJV

¹Now, brethren, concerning the coming of our Lord Jesus Christ and our gathering together to Him, we ask you, ²not to be soon shaken in mind or troubled, either by spirit or by word or by letter, as if from us, as though the day of Christ had come. ³Let no one deceive you by any means; for that Day will not come unless the falling away comes first, and the man of sin is revealed, the son of perdition, ⁴who opposes and exalts himself above all that is called God or that is worshiped, so that he sits as God in the temple of God, showing himself that he is God.

⁵Do you not remember that when I was still with you I told you these things? ⁶And now you know what is restraining, that he may be revealed in his own time. ⁷For the mystery of lawlessness is already at work; only He who now restrains will do so until He is taken out of the way. ⁸And then the lawless one will be revealed, whom the Lord will consume with the breath of His mouth and destroy with the brightness of His coming. ⁹The coming of the lawless one is according to the working of Satan, with all power, signs, and lying wonders, ¹⁰and with all unrighteous deception among those who perish, because they did not receive the love of the truth, that they might be saved. ¹¹And for this reason God will send them strong delusion, that they should believe the lie, ¹²that they all may be condemned who did not believe the truth but had pleasure in unrighteousness.

EXPLORATION

1. Why do you think there is so much confusion, even among Christians, about the "end times"?

2. What has to happen before "the day of Christ" (vv. 2–3 NKJV)?

3. Compare what this passage says about "the man of sin" (v. 3 NKJV) or the "lawless one" (v. 8) with 1 John 4:2–3 and Revelation 13:1–10. What are the distinguishing characteristics of this "Man of Evil" (v. 4 NCV)?

4. What does all this prophecy about the future suggest about the unfolding events of human history?

5. This passage contains the words "deceive" (v. 3 NKJV), "lying" (v. 9), "deception" (v. 10), "delusion" (v. 11), and "lie" (v. 11). What is the message for Paul's readers?

INSPIRATION

God has made it clear. The plague of sin will not cross his shores. Infected souls never walk his streets. *"Unjust people who don't care about God will not be joining in his kingdom. Those who use and abuse each other, use and abuse sex, use and abuse the earth and everything in it, don't qualify as citizens in God's kingdom"* (1 Cor. 6:9–10 MSG). God refuses to compromise the spiritual purity of heaven.

Herein lies the awful fruit of sin. Lead a godless life, and expect a godless eternity. Spend a life telling God to leave you alone, and he will. He'll grant you an existence *"without God and without hope"* (Eph. 2:12). Jesus will *"punish those who reject God and who do not obey the Good News about our Lord Jesus. They will suffer the punishment of eternal destruction, separated from the presence of the Lord and from his glorious might"* (2 Thess. 1:8–9 TEV).

Christ keeps no secrets about hell. His description purposely chills the soul:

A place of darkness (Matt. 8:12)

A fiery furnace (Matt. 13:42)

A place where *"the worm does not die; the fire is never put out"* (Mark 9:48 NCV)

Citizens of hell long to die, but cannot. Beg for water, but receive none. They pass into a dawnless night.

So what can we do? If all have been infected and the world is corrupted, to whom do we turn? Or, to re-ask the great question of Scripture: *"What must I do to be saved?"* (Acts 16:30 NCV). The answer offered then is the answer offered still: *"Put your entire trust in the Master Jesus"* (Acts 16:31 MSG). (From *Come Thirsty* by Max Lucado)

REACTION

6. Though the Bible is emphatic that sin is serious, hell is real, and not all will be saved, many people still do not believe. Why?

7. Scripture declares that a real person called the Antichrist will arise. But even now there is already present in the world an "antichrist spirit." Can you give some examples?

8. How close do you think we are to the "end times"? Why?

9. Paul mentions the reality of false miracles, or signs and wonders done in the power of the evil one. How are we supposed to tell the difference?

10. Who in your life right now seems especially susceptible to spiritual deception?

11. What can and should we do today to get ready for the Lord's return?

LIFE LESSONS

At the risk of sounding cheesy, the truth is that history really is His-story. God is in charge of human events. He doesn't wring his hands while wondering what tomorrow holds. He doesn't react to events, scrambling his angels to deal with unexpected emergencies. No. The fact is our Lord has already written the story of the cosmos. "Breaking news" is old hat in heaven. And the ending? That, too, is a settled issue. For us, this means we can relax. We do not have to fret. Our trust (and our souls) are in the good hands of the author, producer, director, and main character of this unfolding drama called real life. And Scripture assures us that by the time of the final curtain, every question will be answered, and the plot will be clear to all.

DEVOTION

Father, thank you for the truth that our world is not out of control. You have predetermined how all things will unfold. I praise you for being the Lord of the universe and the King of my heart.

For more Bible passages on the evil one, see Genesis 3:4–5; Job 1:9–11; Matthew 13:19; John 8:44; 2 Corinthians 4:3–4; Ephesians 6:12; James 4:7; and 1 Peter 5:8–9.

To complete the books of 1 and 2 Thessalonians during this twelve-part study, read 1 Thessalonians 2:1–12.

JOURNALING

How does God's "Spirit of Truth" keep us from falling victim to the lies of the evil one?

STANDING STRONG

MAX
LUCADO

REFLECTION

Doesn't it seem to be increasingly rare to see people persevere and finally reach their long-term goals? The plan for owning and successfully operating a business, the goal of losing weight or getting into shape, the hope of becoming financially healthy. What causes so many to give up their dreams?

SITUATION

To a young church immersed in godless culture and surrounded by false teachings, Paul writes these words of reminder and challenge. His message? Stand firm. Don't be deceived. Believe and cling stubbornly to the truth. And trust in the Lord's faithfulness and power.

OBSERVATION

Read 2 Thessalonians 2:13–17 from the NCV or the NKJV.

NCV

¹³Brothers and sisters, whom the Lord loves, God chose you from the beginning to be saved. So we must always thank God for you. You are saved by the Spirit that makes you holy and by your faith in the truth. ¹⁴God used the Good News that we preached to call you to be saved so you can share in the glory of our Lord Jesus Christ. ¹⁵So, brothers and sisters, stand strong and continue to believe the teachings we gave you in our speaking and in our letter.

¹⁶May our Lord Jesus Christ himself and God our Father encourage you and strengthen you in every good thing you do and say. God loved us, and through his grace he gave us a good hope and encouragement that continues forever.

NKJV

¹³But we are bound to give thanks to God always for you, brethren beloved by the Lord, because God from the beginning chose you for salvation through sanctification by the Spirit and belief in the truth, ¹⁴to which He called you by our gospel, for the obtaining of the glory of our Lord Jesus Christ. ¹⁵Therefore, brethren, stand fast and hold the traditions which you were taught, whether by word or our epistle.

¹⁶Now may our Lord Jesus Christ Himself, and our God and Father, who has loved us and given us everlasting consolation and good hope by grace, ¹⁷comfort your hearts and establish you in every good word and work.

EXPLORATION

1. When is the last time you truly and deeply sensed the truth that you are loved by God (see v. 13)?

2. Looking back, what are some of the ways God worked in your life to bring you to faith?

3. Paul crams a lot of theology in these few verses. What are some of the reasons he lists that Christians can be thankful?

4. What are some specific ways God encourages and strengthens you (see verse 16)?

5. What has been the most difficult period of your life, and how did you endure that experience?

INSPIRATION

Jesus is honest about the life we are called to lead. There is no guarantee that just because we belong to him we will go unscathed. No promise is found in Scripture that says when you follow the king you are exempt from battle. No, often just the opposite is the case.

How do we survive the battle? How do we endure the fray? . . .

"Those people who keep their faith until the end will be saved" (Matt. 24:13 NCV).

He doesn't say if you succeed you will be saved. Or if you come out on top you will be saved. He says if you endure. An accurate rendering would be, "If you hang in there until the end . . . if you go the distance."

The Brazilians have a great phrase for this. In Portuguese, a person who has the ability to hang in and not give up has *garra*. *Garra* means "claws." What imagery! A person with *garra* has claws which burrow into the side of the cliff and keep him from falling.

So do the saved. They may get close to the edge, they may even stumble and slide. But they will dig their nails into the rock of God and hang on.

I've been told that during the filming of *Ben Hur,* Charlton Heston had trouble learning to drive a chariot (who wouldn't?). With much practice he was finally able to control the vehicle, but still had some doubts. He reportedly explained his concerns to the director Cecil B. DeMille by saying, "I think I can drive the chariot, but I'm not sure I can win the race."

DeMille responded, "You just stay in the race and I'll make sure you win." (From *And the Angels Were Silent* by Max Lucado)

REACTION

6. What specific circumstances in your life right now are making it difficult for you to "stay in the race"?

7. What believer do you admire for his or her ability to persevere?

8. Would you say you are more encouraged or discouraged right now? Why?

9. How would you answer a young Christian who pleaded, "I feel my faith faltering—what are some practical ways I can 'continue to believe the teachings' of Christ" (v. 15 NCV)?

10. Go back through this passage and jot down every description you see about God's nature or activity. Spend a moment reflecting on these characteristics. How does this affect you?

11. In what specific areas of your life (or in the face of what difficulties) do you need to stand stronger and persevere more fiercely?

LIFE LESSONS

The most common New Testament Greek word translated "persevere" in our English Bibles is actually a compound term made up of the Greek verb meaning "to remain" together with the prefix "under." In other words, persevering involves "remaining under" a situation. Think of a weight lifter who bench-presses an enormous weight. It is only under that heavy barbell that he gains muscle and new strength. In the same way, we develop character and faith only when we stay in tough situations. Quitting, running away—these are the habits of those who never reach the goal, who never reach their full potential. Because of Christ, we can do far more than we realize!

DEVOTION

Lord Jesus, forgive my tendency to complain or quit when situations get hard. Teach me to persevere. Remind me, as the apostle Paul once prayed, that "I can do all things through Christ who strengthens me."

For more Bible passages on standing firm, see Joshua 23:8; 2 Kings 22:2; Acts 4:19–20; 1 Corinthians 15:58; Galatians 5:1; Philippians 1:27; Hebrews 12:1; 1 Peter 5:9; and Revelation 3:11.

To complete the books of 1 and 2 Thessalonians during this twelve-part study, read 2 Thessalonians 2:13–17.

JOURNALING

List some people in your life who could use your prayers and your encouragement. Add some specific ways you could come alongside these friends or loved ones to offer hope and help.

THE
IMPORTANCE
OF
INTERCESSION

MAX
LUCADO

REFLECTION

The statistics on prayer are surprising. An overwhelming majority of people—even irreligious people, and even some agnostics!—admit to praying at least occasionally. What do you think motivates most of the prayers that people offer?

SITUATION

Eager to aid the spread of the gospel, facing persecution and convinced of the certainty of the Lord's return to judge the world, Paul requests prayer support from the Christians in Thessalonica. He also prays for them.

OBSERVATION

Read 2 Thessalonians 3:1–5 from the NCV or the NKJV.

NCV

¹And now, brothers and sisters, pray for us that the Lord's teaching will continue to spread quickly and that people will give honor to that teaching, just as happened with you. ²And pray that we will be protected from stubborn and evil people, because not all people believe.

³But the Lord is faithful and will give you strength and will protect you from the Evil One. ⁴The Lord makes us feel sure that you are doing and will continue to do the things we told you. ⁵May the Lord lead your hearts into God's love and Christ's patience.

NKJV

¹Finally, brethren, pray for us, that the word of the Lord may run swiftly and be glorified, just as it is with you, ²and that we may be delivered from unreasonable and wicked men; for not all have faith.

³But the Lord is faithful, who will establish you and guard you from the evil one. ⁴And we have confidence in the Lord concerning you, both that you do and will do the things we command you.

⁵Now may the Lord direct your hearts into the love of God and into the patience of Christ.

EXPLORATION

1. Why doesn't Paul request more specific prayer for a lessening of his troubles?

2. What percentage of your praying revolves around the spread of the gospel?

3. How consistently do you pray for others?

4. This passage contains several references to the Lord's character. Why is an accurate view of God's nature so essential to a healthy prayer life?

5. Describe your personal prayer habits (i.e., the how, what, when, where, and why)?

INSPIRATION

John is old now. He's the silver-haired figure stepping through the jagged rocks on a beach. He's looking for a flat place where he can kneel. It is the Lord's day. And John has come to see his Lord . . .

He is exiled, banished from his friends . . . Cut off. With the stroke of a magistrate's pen he was sentenced to pass his days with no companion, with no church. . . . Rome placed John on Patmos for punishment. Heaven placed John on Patmos for privilege . . .

[A]s he prayed, he . . . saw what no man had ever seen. The same eyes that saw the resurrected Lord now saw heaven open. And for the next few seconds, minutes, or days, John was caught up in the fury and passion of living in the end of times and in the presence of God . . .

The air is full of sounds—earthquakes, trumpets, proclamations, and declarations. From the first word of the angel there is constant activity and non-stop noise until: "There was silence in heaven for about half an hour . . ." (Rev. 8:1 NCV). Strange this sudden reference to minutes. Nothing else is timed . . . Why "half an hour"? Why not fifteen minutes or one hour? I don't know. I don't know if John was literal or symbolic. But I do know that, as an orchestra falls silent at the lifting of the conductor's baton, so heaven hushed when the Lamb opened the seventh seal.

As the first six seals revealed how God acts, the seventh revealed how God listens. Look what happens after the seventh seal is opened.

When the Lamb opened the seventh seal, there was silence in heaven for about half an hour. And I saw the seven angels who stand before God and to whom were given seven trumpets. Another angel came and stood at the altar, holding a golden pan for incense. He was given much incense to offer with the prayers of all God's holy people. The angel put this offering on the golden altar before the throne. The smoke from the incense went up from the angel's hand to God with the prayers of God's holy people. Then the angel filled the incense pan with fire from the altar and threw it on the earth, and there were flashes of lightning, thunder and loud noises, and an earthquake. (8:1–5)

Every song ceased. Every being of the heavenly city hushed. The noise stopped. A sudden stillness fell like a curtain. Why? Why did the Lamb lift his hand for silence? Why did the silver-trumpet voices hush? Because someone was praying. Heaven paused, and Heaven pauses to hear the prayers of . . . someone. A mother for her child. A pastor for a church. A doctor for the diseased. A counselor for the confused. (From *The Great House of God* by Max Lucado)

REACTION

6. How does it impact you to realize that God not only invites your prayer, but also bends low to listen intently to the cries of your heart?

7. It's been said that God does indeed answer every prayer—his response being either "yes," "no," or "wait." How do you typically react when you fail to get a quick "yes" answer from God?

8. Do you think prayer changes our circumstances more, or us more? Why?

9. God could have ordered the world in vastly different ways. He certainly doesn't need us. Why do you think he elected to incorporate this "system" of prayer?

10. Who are some people that you could approach about being prayer partners with you?

II. Make a list of people in your life who could use your faithful prayer support. Start with your small group. Solicit specific requests from these friends and loved ones.

LIFE LESSONS

A rich prayer life always begins with a right view of God. The person who believes that God is uncaring or unfair will never be motivated to seek him. At the same time, the individual who thinks of God as a cosmic genie or celestial St. Nick will also end up frustrated. But the Christian who sees God as he is—a good, wise, powerful, and always faithful Father—that person *will* be eager to pour out his or her heart to God. And here's one more truth: The more deeply we taste his saving and sustaining grace, the more we will pray for others to meet him and experience his life-changing presence and peace.

DEVOTION

Father, give me a selfless heart. Make me a prayer warrior, always mindful of others, always bringing their needs before your throne.

For more Bible passages on praying for others, see 1 Samuel 7:8; 12:19; 1 Kings 13:6; Acts 8:24; Romans 15:30; Ephesians 6:19; 1 Thessalonians 5:25; and Hebrews 13:18.

To complete the books of 1 and 2 Thessalonians during this twelve-part study, read 2 Thessalonians 3:1–5.

JOURNALING

Write out a short prayer for each of three people in your life who are facing great struggles.

WORK

MAX
LUCADO

REFLECTION

Even our bumper stickers reveal our culture's disdain for work: "Work fascinates me . . . I can sit and look at it for hours!" "I owe, I owe. It's off to work I go." Thinking back over your years of employment, what have been your worst jobs? Your best jobs?

SITUATION

Confused by the claims of some that the end of the world was at hand, some Thessalonian believers had quit their jobs to wait for the return of Christ. Paul corrects these wrong beliefs and behaviors, and in the process, gives us some helpful hints about working in a way that pleases God.

OBSERVATION

Read 2 Thessalonians 3:6–18 from the NCV or the NKJV.

NCV

⁶Brothers and sisters, by the authority of our Lord Jesus Christ we command you to stay away from any believer who refuses to work and does not follow the teaching we gave you. ⁷You yourselves know that you should live as we live. We were not lazy when we were with you. ⁸And when we ate another person's food, we always paid for it. We worked very hard night and day so we would not be an expense to any of you. ⁹We had the right to ask you to help us, but we worked to take care of ourselves so we would be an example for you to follow. ¹⁰When we were with you, we gave you this rule: "Anyone who refuses to work should not eat."

¹¹We hear that some people in your group refuse to work. They do nothing but busy themselves in other people's lives. ¹²We command those people and beg them in the Lord Jesus Christ to work quietly and earn their own food. ¹³But you, brothers and sisters, never become tired of doing good.

¹⁴If some people do not obey what we tell you in this letter, then take note of them. Have nothing to do with them so they will feel ashamed. ¹⁵But do not treat them as enemies. Warn them as fellow believers.

16Now may the Lord of peace give you peace at all times and in every way. The Lord be with all of you.

17I, Paul, end this letter now in my own handwriting. All my letters have this to show they are from me. This is the way I write.

18The grace of our Lord Jesus Christ be with you all.

NKJV

6But we command you, brethren, in the name of our Lord Jesus Christ, that you withdraw from every brother who walks disorderly and not according to the tradition which he received from us. 7For you yourselves know how you ought to follow us, for we were not disorderly among you; 8nor did we eat anyone's bread free of charge, but worked with labor and toil night and day, that we might not be a burden to any of you, 9not because we do not have authority, but to make ourselves an example of how you should follow us.

10For even when we were with you, we commanded you this: If anyone will not work, neither shall he eat. 11For we hear that there are some who walk among you in a disorderly manner, not working at all, but are busybodies. 12Now those who are such we command and exhort through our Lord Jesus Christ that they work in quietness and eat their own bread.

13But as for you, brethren, do not grow weary in doing good. 14And if anyone does not obey our word in this epistle, note that person and do not keep company with him, that he may be ashamed. 15Yet do not count him as an enemy, but admonish him as a brother.

16Now may the Lord of peace Himself give you peace always in every way. The Lord be with you all.

17The salutation of Paul with my own hand, which is a sign in every epistle; so I write.

18The grace of our Lord Jesus Christ be with you all. Amen.

EXPLORATION

1. What should be our response to lazy Christians?

2. Paul describes his own work habits, holding them up as a model (vv. 7–10). How would your coworkers describe your personal work habits?

3. How, if at all, could the principles in this passage be applied to the question of "public welfare"?

4. Why does a believer's work ethic matter so much?

5. Verses 14–15 raise the issue of confronting others. Do you do this? When?

INSPIRATION

Consider these sobering statistics:

One-third of Americans say, "I hate my job."

Two-thirds of your fellow citizens labor in the wrong career.

Others find employment success, but no satisfaction.

Most suicides occur on Sunday nights.

Most heart attacks occur on Monday mornings.

Many people dread their work! Countless commuters begrudge the 83,000 hours their jobs take from their lives. If you're one of them, what can you do?

Change careers? Perhaps. Find one that better fits your design. But until you change, how do you survive? You still have bills to pay and obligations to meet. The problem might be less the occupation and more the outlook toward. Before you change professions, try this: change your attitude toward your profession.

Jesus's word for frustrated workers can be found in the fifth chapter of Luke's gospel . . . Random pockets of people populate the Galilean seacoast today. But in the days of Christ, it swarmed, an ant bed of activity. Peter, Andrew, James, and John made their living catching and selling fish. Like other fishermen, they worked the night shift, when cool water brought the game to the surface. And, like other fishermen, they knew the drudgery of a fishless night.

While Jesus preaches, they clean nets. And as the crowd grows, Christ has an idea.

He noticed two boats tied up. The fishermen had just left them and were scrubbing out their nets. He climbed into the boat that was [Peter's] and asked him to put out a little from the shore. Sitting there, using the boat for a pulpit, he taught the crowd. (Luke 5:2–3 MSG)

Jesus claims Peter's boat. He doesn't *request* the use of it. Christ doesn't fill out an application or ask permission; he simply boards the boat and begins to preach.

He can do that, you know. All boats belong to Christ. Your boat is where you spend your day, make your living, and to a large degree live your life. The taxi you drive, the horse stable you clean, the dental office you manage, the family you feed and transport—this is your boat. Christ shoulder-taps us and reminds:

"You drive my truck."

"You preside in my courtroom."

"You work on my job site."

"You serve my hospital wing."

To us all, Jesus says, "Your work is my work." (From *Cure for the Common Life* by Max Lucado)

REACTION

6. How would it change your daily experience if you began seeing your job as a way of serving Christ, as a place to shine for him?

7. Do you think laziness is "contagious"? Why?

8. Arriving late, leaving early, surfing the Net on company time—what are some other common ways Christian workers fail to work in an exemplary fashion?

9. How important is it for parents to teach their children how to work hard and with excellence?

10. What's the right response by a community of faith toward the believer who refuses to support his or her family?

11. What specific changes do you need to make in your work habits, effective immediately?

LIFE LESSONS

Many Christians believe that work itself is evil and part of the divine curse on sin. Not so! God worked in creating the world, and called the fruit of his labors "good." Not only that, but before the fall of humankind, in that perfect environment of Eden, God commissioned Adam to work (Gen. 2:15). The fact is, when we work with excellence and creativity, we imitate God. As believers, the workplace is one of our primary arenas in which to model the difference Christ makes. Treating coworkers or employees well. Showing respect to superiors. Doing what we're told. Meeting deadlines. Going the extra mile. Giving 100 percent. Staying focused. Solving problems. Conducting all our efforts with integrity. All of these rare responses provide a great platform for the gospel.

DEVOTION

Father, no matter what I say or claim to believe, if I don't exhibit a changed life in my workplace, my faith is an obstacle to unbelievers. Give me the courage to look closely at my work habits, and the grace to bring them in line with your Word.

For more Bible passages on being a God-honoring worker, see Genesis 3:19; Proverbs 14:23; 25:13; 27:18; Ecclesiastes 9:10; Ephesians 4:28; Colossians 3:22; 1 Timothy 6:1; Titus 2:9; and 1 Peter 2:18.

To complete the books of 1 and 2 Thessalonians during this twelve-part study, read 2 Thessalonians 3:6–18.

JOURNALING

List ten qualities that you think Jesus looks for in a worker.

Lucado Life Lesson Series

Revised and updated, the Lucado Life Lessons series is perfect for small group or individual use and includes intriguing questions that will take you deeper into God's Word.

THOMAS NELSON
Since 1798

Available at your local Christian Bookstore.